The 50 Greatest British Sitcoms

Roger Barker

Contents

Introduction

Britain is famous for its sitcoms. Many have been been made and numerous sitcoms are regarded as all time classic British television shows. In the past sitcoms were ubiquitous on television - particularly in the 1970s - making up a key part of programme schedules. In later years sitcoms have become rarer, but are still shown. It is common for comedies today to have a modern take on the sitcom and have no laughter track and be almost like a comedy drama.

What are the greatest British sitcoms? This is a subjective opinion as people have different senses of humour; this book is the author's opinion, taking into account some other factors such as impact on popular culture, production values and so forth. There is a consensus on the best British sitcoms. These appear on greatest sitcom lists, or a critically acclaimed today. Another way to determine to the British sitcom can be to note which old sitcoms are repeated on British television channels.

Hopefully this book will be of interest to those interested in British sitcoms and comedy and hopefully the reader will be introduced to some new comedy classics.

The Sitcoms

Allo 'Allo!

BBC

Written by Jeremy Lloyd and David Croft

Eighty five episodes over nine series.

First shown from 30 December 1982 - 14 December 1992.

Stars:

Gordon Kaye as Rene Artois
Carmen Silvera as Edith Melba Artois
Hilary Minster as Major-General bon Klinkerhoffen
Guy Siner as Lietenant Gruber
Kim Hartman as Helga Geerhart
Kirsten Cooke as Michelle
Vicki Michelle as Yvette

It is 1940 and World War 2. The French town of Nouvion is occupied by the Nazis. Local cafe owner Rene Artois is a reluctant member of the local French resistance group.

Another charming sitcom from Jeremy Lloyd and David Croft who wrote Are You Being Served together. Croft wrote other historical comedies It

Ain't Half Hot Mum, Hi-de-Hi! and Dad's Army with Jimmy Perry.

The series is perhaps in poor taste having the SS, Gestapo and other Nazi figures as comedy characters. But it is in the British tradition of lampooning authority figures. The long running sitcom had a series of running plot lines through the period of World War II. The character of Rene gave a recap of the story at the start of each episode.

The series has a selection of rather cheesy jokes and over the top characters. It is laced with slapstick and innuendo. This creates a classic British comedy. The characters have many catchphrases of their own. For example French resistance leader Michelle says "I will say this only once.". One memorable is Arthur Bostrom as a British spy posing as a French policeman. When speaking French he (in English with a comedy accent of course) often mispronounces words resulting in double entrendes or innuendo. For example instead of Good Morning he says Good Moaning. The long suffering Rene is wonderfully played by Gordon Kaye, and there is a huge cast of actors in the show who are superb.

The show was a spoof of war films and some of the 70s British dramas about wartime resistance groups such as Secret Army. A classic show which is almost like watching a great stage show.

Are You Being Served?

BBC

Written by Jeremy Lloyd and David Croft; some
episodes written by Michael Knowles and John
Chapman
Seventy episodes over ten series

First shown from 8 September 1972 –1 April 1985

Stars:

John Inman as Mr Humphries
Molie Sugden as Betty Slocombe
Wendy Richard as Shirley Brahms
Frank Thornton as Captain Peacock
Nicholas Smith as Cuthbert Rumbold
Trevor Bannister as Mr Lucas
Arthur Brough as Ernest Grainger
Harold Bennett as Young Mr Grace
Larry Martyn as Mr Mash
Arthur English as Mr Harman

The show is set in the ladies' and men's'
department of the London flagship Grace Brothers
department store chain.

A classic and long running sitcom with many
iconic characters.

There is gay stereotype Mr Humphries played
wonderfully by John Inman, with his catchphrase

"I'm free", when asked if he is free to deal with a customer. Mollie Sugden plays the feisty Mrs Slocombe. Wendy Richard is charming as young cockney sales assistant Shirley. Trevor Bannister plays the cheeky womanising Mr Lucas. Arthur Brough plays the elderly and grumpy sales assistant Mr Grainger. Frank Thornton plays Captain Peacock a pompous middle manager in the department. Nicholas Smith plays Mr Rumbold another pomp's manager. Larry Martyn and Arthur English play maintenance men. Harold Bennett plays Young Mr Grace (a joke as he is elderly) the tight fisted store owner who always has a rather young secretary.

Due to the long running nature of the series some actors left the series or passed away. Arthur Brough died after the 5th series. Harold Bennett died before the ninth series. Trevor Bannister left after series 7 to work on other projects.

The series has a good ensemble cast. One of the keys to the show's success is that it almost like a stage play with a large set making up the department store. There are often musical or variety numbers involving the cast. One amusing regular item is dinner at the canteen as the fare is always awful. The show is full or slapstick and double ententes. Mre Slocombe refers to her cat as my pussy causing some confusion and almost creating a single entente! In between the rather broad humour there are some quite decent plots such as characters wanting to gain promotion or fearing the sack.

There is a lot of commentary on the class system with some members of staff seeing themselves as above others and being overly obsessed with etiquette.

The show is a cult programme in the US after it was shown on PBS in the 1980s.

A film was released in 1977 where the staff go on holiday to the fictional Spanish resort of Costa Plonka. This is entertaining but takes place on a large set of a hotel lobby and garden/dining area: it was based on a play. It would have been nice to see the characters in outdoor locations in London in a film. If the 70 episodes and film are not enough there was an Australian version made. Two series of sixteen episodes were made between 1980-81. There were Australian versions of the characters (with different names) and John Inman starred as Mr Humphries.

After the show ended in 1985, a spin off was made in 1992. Two series and twelve episodes were made. The premise of the series was that the characters' Grace Brothers pension fund is a country manor house called Millstone Manor. They are not allowed to sell the house. They decide to turn it into a hotel. Mollie Sugden, Frank Thornton, John Inman and Wendy Richard returned in a pleasant spin off to Are You Being Served.

Another show of interest to Are You Being Served? fans is the 1977 sitcom Odd Man Out.

This is a vehicle for John Inman where he plays the owner of a seaside rock (which is a candy) factory. It is a wonderful sitcom in the mould the Cary On films. Sadly only seven episodes were made.

Blackadder

BBC

Written by Ben Elton and Richard Curtis

Twenty four episodes over four series

First shown between 15th June 1983-2nd November 1989

Stars:

Rowan Atkinson as Edmund Blackadder
Tony Robinson as Baldrick
Tim McInnerny as Percy/Captain Darling/various
Hugh Laurie as Prince Regent/ Lieutenant George/various
Stephen Fry as Lord Melchett/ General Melchett/various
Miranda Richardson as Queen Elizabeth I/various

The series shows Edmund Blackadder and his assistant Baldrick and their descendants in in different historical periods. In the last three series Blackkadder is very clever and manipulating but normally having to work for a less than intelligent authority figure. He assistant by the bumbling and foolish Baldrick. The series includes great humour and dialogue, often based around sarcasm and great comic lines and a fun use of history.

An iconic show which is often near the list of polls of best British sitcom. There are four series from different time periods.

The first series The Black Adder ran was first shown in 1983. This series was set in 1495. In an alternate history plotline, Richard III has won the Battle of Bosworth Field but is murdered and replaced by Richard IV. Blackader is Edmund, the Duke of Edinburgh Richard IV's second son. Is this first series Blackadder is not a confident character and different from the rest of the series. As a result it is the weakest of the series.

The second series Blackadder II was broadcast in 1986. This is set during the reign of Queen Elizabeth from 1558-1603. The Queen is wonderfully played by Miranda Richardson in a comically childish but scheming way. Edmund, Lord Blackadder is an aristocrat who attempt to win favour of the Queen. He lives with his servant Baldrick who is not very intelligent and the buffoonish Lord Percy. Blackadder's rival is the Queen's assistant Lord Melchett. This is a classic series with six memorable episodes. The idea of making Blackadder intelligent and charismatic and making Baldrick an idiot makes this better than the first series.

The third series is called Blackadder the Third and was first shown in 1987. It is set in the Regency period in the late 18th and early 19th century. E. Blackadder Esquire is butler to George the Prince Regent and Prince of Wales. He is again assisted by Baldrick. The Prince is spoiled and idiotic. The series has the usual fun plots and guest stars. One nice addition is Mrs Miggins played by Helen Atkinson Wood. She runs Mrs. Miggins' coffee house which is frequented by the characters.

The fourth series from 1989 is Blackadder Goes Fourth. Set in 1917 on the Western Front in World War 1, it has British soldiers including Captain Blackadder, Private Baldrick, Lieutenant George (Hugh Laurie) and General Melchett. Tim McInnerny plays Captain Darling. This has the usual great plots and lines and many memorable moments. It is a great comment on World War 1. The series is slightly darker than other Blackadder series and World War 1 was an especially bleak war. The last episode is quite moving and is considered to be a classic television episode.

Blackadder's Christmas Carol was first shown at Christmas 1988. It is a spin on A Christmas Carol and as one would expect a charming and very funny one off episode.

A vintage, extremely well made series with many classic moments. Which is the best series? Critical opinion would probably say Blackadder Goes Fourth, but I have a soft spot for Blackadder II.

Bless This House

ITV

Written by Vince Powell and Harry Driver

Sixty five episodes over six series.

First shown from 2 February 1971-22 April 1976

Stars:

Sidney James as Sid Abbott.
Diana Coupland as Jean Abbott
Robin Stewart as Mike Abbott.
Sally Geeson as Sally Abbott
Anthony Jackson as Trevor Lewis
Patsy Rowlands as Betty Lewis.

Sid Abbott lives with his wife Diana and children Mike and Sally in a London suburb. Next door live friends Trevor and Betty Lewis.

A simple traditional British sitcom with British comedy legend Sid James. Sid is a salesman and his character is another incarnation of his traditional Sid James character - a bit of a rogue who likes a drink and has a great sense of humour. Although in this show Sid is more of a family man unlike many of his Carry On roles. Their children are in their late teens and interested in the permissive society and left wing protests. This provides comedy as Sid and Jean are out of touch with them.

The series follows a basic British sitcom template as regards characters and plots, But the charm of James and the cast makes it a classic sitcom.

A classic film version was made in 1972, which had some cast changes. A seventh series and another film was planned. But sadly Sid James died in 1976.

Bottom

BBC

Written by Adrian Edmondson and Rik Mayall

Eighteen episodes over three series.

First shown from 17th September 1991 –10th April 1995

Stars:

Rik Mayall as Richard Richard
Adrian Edmondson as Eddie Hitler

Richard and Eddie live in squalid flat in Hammersmith in London. Unemployed and socially inept, they come up with bizarre schemes to make money or attract women.

A surreal comedy from alternative comedy duo Mayall and Edmondson. The series has the duo's usual over the top characters, often lavatory humour and comedy fights. They are great characters and who can resist Mayall playing one of his crazed characters. The fact that such a thin situation can be turned into an entertaining sitcom that ran for three series is testament to the comedy skills and charisma of Mayall and Edmondson. There are lots of fun plots and memorable scenes and lines.

The show has elements of absurdist theatre in it; Edmondson thought up the idea for the programme when he and Mayalll were appearing in a production of absurdist play Waiting for Godot.

A film was made in 1997 called Guest House Paradiso which is a bit too surreal and not as much fun as the series.

Several successful stage productions of the series were made which were filmed as work as extra episodes/films.

Butterflies

BBC

Written by Carla Lane

Thirty episodes over four series

First shown from 10 November 1978-19 October 1983.
Stars:

Wendy Craig as Ria Parkinson
Geoffrey Palmer as Ben Parkinson
Nicholas Lyndhurst as Adam Parkinson
Andrew Hall as Russel Parkinson

The Parkinson as a well off middle class family living in Cheltenham in England.. Although still in love with her dentist husband housewife Ria is unhappy with her routine life - having a mid life crisis - and yearns for something more.

An interesting sitcom from Carla Lane. Ria is a traditional stay at home housewife and bored with life. She considers an affair with businessman friend Leonard who she meets in parks for walks. She also confides in Leonard's chauffeur Thomas. Ria's husband Ben has traditional values and conflicts with his teenage son's modern views on drugs and pregnancy outside marriage.

The titles refer to Ben's hobby of Lepidopterology - the study of Butterflies. One memorable part of the series is Ria's awful cooking skills. She prepares awful meals which are politely eaten by her family.

A charming comedy about the boredom of a middle aged housewife.

Colin's Sandwich

BBC

Written by Terry Kyan and Paul Smith
Twelve episodes over two series.

First shown between 18 October 1988 - 16
February 1990.

Stars:

Mel Smith as Colin Watkins
Louisa Rix as Jenny Anderson
Tony Haase as Trevor
Mike Grady as Des
Nicholas Ball as Alan Hunter

Colin Watkins for British Rail in the complaints
department. He is bored by his job and wishes to
become a horror writer.

A great comedy starring British comedy legend
Mel Smith. It is a vehicle for Smith's comic
persona with his facial expressions and sarcastic
sense of humour. Colin is intelligent but neurotic
and stuck in a boring job, wishing to pursue a
career as a writer. Colin has many monologues
and there is often a voice over of Colin's thoughts.

Colin is a very sympathetic character with his
battles against the more mundane and banal
conventions and rituals of society. The comedy

comes from his behaviour in reaction to routine situations and many of the somewhat absurd situations he finds himself in. One fun ongoing story is Colin's attempts to get a short story and film script competed by publisher Alan Langley (played by the excellent Nicholas Ball) who is constantly stringing him along, asking for rewrites etc.

A very interesting sitcom with a good range of characters and plots - some dramatic - which has been a little forgotten today. Also a great late 80s period piece.

Dad's Army

BBC

Written by Jimmy Perry and David Croft

Eighty episodes over nine series.

First shown between 31 July 1968-13 November 1977.

Stars:

Arthur Lowe Captain George Mainwaring
Sergeant Arthur Wilson (John Le Mesurier),
Lance Corporal Jack Jones (Clive Dunn)
Private James Frazer (John Laurie)
Private Joe Walker (James Beck),

Private Charles Godfrey (Arnold Ridley)
Private Frank Pike (Ian Lavender)
ARP Chief Warden William Hodges (Bill Pertwee)
The Reverend Timothy Farthing (Frank Williams),
the

In 1940 Britain is under threat of invasion from
Nazi Germany. In the southern English coastal
town of Walmington on Sea a local Home Guard
army detachment made up of older people and
others ineligible for military service is formed.
An extremely iconic and popular programme. The
series has an ensemble cast of memorable funny
characters.

The comedy comes from these group of misfits
and mostly elderly men being formed into a
fighting unit to resist the Nazis.

These include pompous platoon leader Captain
Mainwaring, played excellently by Arthur Lowe.
The buffoonish Jones, played by Clive Dunn who is
made up to look older. Sergeant Wilson is an
upper class man who is Mainwaring's deputy but
obviously intellectually his superior. Frazer is a
black marketeer and spiv. Private Pike is a daft
young man who has not been called up to the
army because of a health issue. Mainwaring often
calls him a "stupid boy" when he has done
something wrong.

There are an array of other characters such as
vicars, army officers, all nicely depicted. The
series has great production values, being filmed

near Thetford in Norfolk. It has many wonderful well written World War related plots and memorable lines and scenes with some dramatic moments.

A memorable theme song, a pastiche of British World War 2 songs and a great opening and ending title sequence complete a classic show.

A film was made in 1971 which is quite good, although the cast and writers were unhappy with certain changes to the style and casting of the tv series made by the film company.

Dear John

BBC

Written by John Sullivan

Two series of fourteen episodes.

First shown from 17 February 1986 –21 December 1987

Stars:

Ralph Bates as John Lacey
Belinda Lang as Kate
Peter Denyer as Ralph Dring
Peter Blake as Kirk St Moritz

John Lacey is a secondary school teacher. His wife has left him for best friend Mike. John is living in a bedsit, paying the mortgage on his former home. He has a son Toby who he sees once a week. He joins a support group for divorcees called the 1-2-1 Singles Club where he meets an eccentric group of characters.

A wonderful sitcom from John Sullivan, the writer of Only Fools and Horses and numerous other sitcoms. John is played well by Ralph Bates. The scenes at the divorcee singles group are integral to the program. There are great characters such as Kirk St Moritz. Kirk is a confident personality played by Peter Blake; there is a deeper story to his character though which is revealed in the series. The rather strange nerdy Ralph, the seemingly tough but troubled Kate and others are funny characters.

The show is bittersweet with many characters having problems, but the viewer cares about the characters. The series has been rather forgotten, not repeated very often on British channels in the same way numerous other British comedies are.

An American version also called Dear John was made which ran from 1988-92. This starred Judd Hirsch as John.

Duty Free

ITV

Written by Eric Chappell

Twenty-two episodes over three series.

First shown from 13 February 1984- 25 December 1986.

Stars:

Keith Barron as David Pearce
Gwen Taylor Amy Pearce
Joanna Van Gyseghem as Linda Cochran
Neil Stacy as Robert Cochran
Carlos Douglas as Carlos the Waiter

Two British couples meet holidaying in Marbella in Spain. The Pearces are more working class, the Cochrans more middle class. David Pearce and Linda Cochran start an affair.

A charming romantic farce from Eric Chappell. There is a great ongoing storyline and lots of pleasant plots involving the English couples on holiday. The four main characters are superb and have some great lines. There is little outside location footage with the series being filmed in a studio in England. But the series works as a type of stage play. The series was very popular when it was first shown gaining high viewing figures.

The series was based on Chappell's stage play We're Strangers Here.

Ever Decreasing Circles

BBC

Written by John Esmonde and Bob Larbey

Twenty seven episodes over four series

First shown from 29 January 1984 – 24 December 1989

Stars:

Richard Bryers as Martin Bryce
Penelope Wilton as Ann Bryce
Peter Egan as Paul Ryman
Stanley Lebor as Howard Hughes
Geraldine Newman as Hilda Hughes

Martin Bryce is an obsessive man who likes to think he is at the centre of community life. He is married to Ann. His ordered life is ruined somewhat when charming Cambridge educated hairdresser Paul moves next door.

A wonderful sitcom with great depth. There is a strange, surreal atmosphere to what is ostensibly a traditional British middle class sitcom.

Martin a great character who may seem unsympathetic but is shown to just be trying to deal with life with his obsessiveness. The show is a great satire of suburban communities and their various committees and clubs. The charming Paul who makes everything - sports, humour, business look easy is a source of envy for the very serious Martin which provides the comedy.

A rather strange part of the show are slightly eccentric Howard and Hilda Hughes who are nonetheless a key part of the show. Penelope Wilton is wonderful as Ann who loves Martin is is one of the few sensible people in the show.

A very interesting comedy with a good atmosphere.

Ricky Gervais stated that this is one of his favourite comedies.

The Fall and Rise of Reginald Perrin

BBC

Written by David Nobbs

Twenty one episodes over three series.

First shown from 8 September 1976-24 January 1979.

Stars:

Leonard Rossiter as Reginald Perrin
Pauline Yates as Elizabeth Perrin
David Warwick as Mark Perrin
Sally-Jane Spencer as Linda Patterson
Sue Nicholls as Joan Greengross
John Barron as CJ

Middle aged Reginald Perrin lives in a London
suburb and commutes every day to his tedious
job as a sales executive at Sunshine Desserts. He
starts to daydream and behave erratically.

A famous sitcom adapted by David Nobbs from his
novel. Perrin is bored with his dull job, commute
and life and decides to make some bizarre
changes after a nervous breakdown. Many people
in real life stuck in the same situation dream of
doing the same thing. Although the show is quite
surreal at times it remain rooted in reality which
helps the success of the sitcom.

There is a great cast of characters: CJ Perrin's
eccentric boss with his business cliches, David and
Tony enthusiastic sales managers creeping around
the boss and Elizabeth Perrin's charming normal
wife.

A wonderful satire on British work and society
with many funny moments - helped by the
comedy acting talents of Leonard Rossiter.

A sequel series The Legacy Of Reginald Perrin was

made in 1996 without Rossiter who had passed
away.

Fawlty Towers

BBC

Written by John Cleese and Connie Booth.

Two series of six episodes.

First shown between 19September 1975-25
October 1979.

Stars:

John Cleese as Basil Fawlty
Prunella Scales as Sybil Fawlty
Connie booth as Polly Sherman
Andrew Sachs as Manuel
Ballard Berkely as Major Gowan
Brian Hall as Terry Hughes

Basil Fawlty runs a small hotel in the English
coastal town of Torquay. He wants his hotel to be
of a higher class and attract guests from the
upper classes, but this is made impossible by the
lower class of his guests and his own mistakes
and those of the staff in running the hotel. He is
henpecked by his wife and has to deal with the
incompetent Manuel, a waiter from Barcelona.
Basil gets into bizarre situations after things

invariably go wrong during the running of the hotel, and gets into numerous arguments with his guests.

A well regarded sitcom that is often mentioned as being the best ever British one. Only 12 episodes were made to ensure the quality of the series. John Cleese stated that he would spend months on each episode to get it right. This means that the series consists of twelve wonderful cogent episodes with memorable scenes and characters.

Basil is a classic character. Sarcastic, witty and eccentric and played well by Cleese. He has to go to bizarre lengths to cover something up from hotel guests and his wife - such as a dead hotel guest or a rat in the hotel. This leads to farcical situations and Basil becoming increasingly erratic and cracking up. Andrew Sachs plays a classic character in Spanish waiter Manuel, a buffoonish character with a rudimentary command of English who is often making mistakes. Ballard Berkely memorably plays the Major a stock character in British comedy. The elderly Major is often in a World of his own.

Basil has to deal with guests who irritate him such as working class guests trying to bring women to their rooms and sarcastic old ladies with hearing aids that do not work. Connie Booth plays waitress Polly who often tries to help (unsuccessfully) extricate him from a bizarre situation.

Prunella Scales is Basil's wife who dominates Basil and he is often scared of her. Sybil steps in to tun the hotel professionally at times and easily clear up Basil's problems.

Cleese's inspiration for the character was a hotel owner by the name of Donald Sinclair. Cleese and the Monty Python team stayed at Sinclair's Gleneagles Hotel in Torquay in 1970 and Cleese was amused how Sinclair hated the guests.

Fresh Fields

ITV

Written by John Chapman

Twenty seven episodes over four series.

First shown between 7th Mach 1984-23rd October 1986

Stars:

Julia McKenzie as Hester Fields
Anton Rogers   as William Fields
Ann Beach as Sonia Barrett
Fanny Rowe as Nancy Penrose
Debby Cumming as Emma Fields
Ballard Berkeley as Guy Penrose
Daphne Oxenford as Miss Denham
John Arthur as John Barrett

Hester and William Fields are a middle aged middle class couple living in a suburb of London. William is an accountant, Hester is a housewife who is exploring new hobbies, jobs and business ideas. Hester's mother Nancy lives in the house in a granny flat.

Another typical British middle class sitcom with the husband working and the wife at home. The show might seem bland, but it is wonderful to watch and has great comedy in the farce tradition. The show is helped by Anton Rodgers and Julia Mackenzie who give absolutely charming comic performances. Ann Bleach is funny as Sonia constantly coming around and borrowing food and drink annoying William. Her catchphrase when she comes round is a good one: "it's only Sonia". Ballard Berkeley gives a typically funny performance as Hester's father. Fanny Rowe as Nancy is a great addition. The theme tune is very memorable. Fun plots and a great setting make this cosy sitcom and one of the best in the middle class suburban genre.

A continuation of the show with a different setting was made in the guise of French Fields. Three series of nineteen episodes were made between 1989-91 - three years after Fresh Fields. As the name suggests in this episode the Fields move to France after William's work has him move to Calais. It is still a charming show with great episodes but the French setting does not quite work as well as the London backdrop. Also Nancy Rowe and Ballard Berkeley had died before French

Fields and are missed.

George & Mildred

ITV

Written by Brian Cooke and Johnnie Mortimer

Thirty eight episodes over five series

First shown from 6th December 1976-25 December 1979

Stars:

Brian Murphy as George Roper
Yootha Joyce as Mildred Roper
Norman Eshley as Jeffrey Fourmile
Sheila Fearn as Ann Fourmile
Nicholas Bond-Owen as Tristram Fourmile

George and Mildred Roper have sold their London boarding house and decide to move to the upmarket London suburb of Hampton Wick. Mildred hoped to become a figure in the community. Next door live the snobbish Jeffrey Fourmile, his wife Ann and son Tristram.

A spin off from the popular Man About the House sitcom which had the Ropers as landlords in a boarding house. The humour is based on the bickering Ropers. George is uncouth and work-shy and tries to avoid sex with Mildred. Mildred dreams of mixing in local social circles. Mildred has a number of amusing quips aimed at George.

The show is not dark and one can see the Ropers are close and understand each other which is a great aspect of the characters.

Next door is the snobbish Jeffrey who takes a dislike to George's working class manner. Tristram forms a friendship with George and Ann is friendly and chides Jeffrey for his behaviour.

This is a classic traditional British sitcom with great characters in George and Mildred. The Fourmiles are a good addition and make the show

A film was made in 1980. This is disappointing featuring a weak doppleganger related plot at a London hotel. A sixth series was in production when Yootha Joyce sadly died.

The Goodies

BBC

Written by Tim Brooke Taylor, Graeme Garden and Bill Oddie

Seventy six episodes over nine series.

First shown from 8th November 1970- 13th

February 1982

Stars:

Tim Brooke Taylor
Graeme Garden
Bill Oddie

Three men hire themselves out for jobs. They have the tagline "We Do Anything, Anytime, Anywhere".

A wonderful mixture of sitcom and sketch comedy. The trio are based in a Cricklewood office and there are lots of sequences based there. They are given strange jobs which is used as a pretext for lots of off the wall, surreal and strange slapstick comedy.

The series has a lot of satire and parody in it on world events. The humour was quite radical politically on occasion, which sometimes caused controversy. A very inventive series and classic series.

The series is in the same vein as Monty Python, and the Goodies stars wrote and appeared in numerous comedy shows with Python members early in their careers.

The Good Life

BBC

Written by John Esmonde and Bob Larbey

Four series, thirty episodes in total.

First shown from 4th April 1975 – 10th June 1978

Stars:

Richard Briers as Tom Good
Felicity Kendal as Barbara Good
Penelope Keith as Margo Leadbetter
Paul Eddington as Jeremy "Jerry" Leadbetter

Tom Good works as a draughtsman for a company that makes plastic toys for cereal packets. On his 40th birthday he decides to give up his job and adopt at self-sufficient lifestyle at his suburban house. Tom lives with his wife Barbara. Neighbours and friends are Jerry Leadbetter - a work colleague of Tom's, and his wife Margo.

A very popular and well regarded sitcom. Tom has a midlife crisis and decides to ditch his job and commute to work. He adopts a self sufficient lifestyle farming in his garden to provide food and making other household items. The comedy stems from the fact that he is doing this in his suburban house rather than on a piece of land in the countryside. The Goods life in a quite affluent area and their behaviour appals neighbour Margo who is a conservative and sees herself as a pillar of local middle class society. But she is friends with the Goods and one of the charms of the programme is how she accepts the Goods lifestyle even though she finds it confusing and probably extremely annoying.

The cast is excellent and the characters have gone on to be iconic. Special praise must be given to Penelope Keith as the domineering Margaret Thatcher esque Margo. Paul Eddington is wonderful as always as the charming Jerry. Peter Bowles was originally cast as Jerry. But he was working on another project so could not appear. Bowles later worked with Keith on To the Manor Born. Felicity Kendall is marvellous as Barbara and her and Briers work very well together. The chemistry between these four make the show.

The programme mirrored the rise of Green issues and self sufficiency in 1970s Britain, and the show has been cited as a reason for the increase in popularity of these ideas. A classic Christmas special was shown at Christmas 1977.

Hancock's Half Hour

BBC

Written by Ray Galton and Alan Simpson.

Sixty three episodes over seven series.

First shown from the 7th July 1956-30th June 1961.

Stars:

Tony Hancock
Sid James
Hugh Lloyd,
Kenneth Williams
Hattie Jacques

Actor/comedian Tony Hancock lives in East Cheam in London. His friend is criminal and con man Sid.

A television adaption of the classic radio series. The radio series and subsequent television series was an early sitcom. Beforehand comedy shows were a mainly mix of sketches and musical interludes. The series has some memorable episodes and many great plots. It is a great vehicle for Tony Hancock with his facial expressions and wonderful comic timing and delivery. He has many wonderful lines supplied by Galton and Simpson. Hancock is simply brilliant as a pompous dreamer whose plans always seem to fail through bad luck or because of Sid. Sid James is a joy playing a character in the guise of his crooked Sid persona.

Unfortunately around twenty six episodes are missing.

Hi-De-Hi!

BBC

Written by Jimmy Perry and David Croft

Fifty eight episodes over nine series.

First shown between 1st January 1980-30th January 1988.

Stars:
Simon Cadell as Professor Jeffrey Fairbrother
Paul Shane as Ted Bovis
Ruth Madoc as Gladys Pugh
Jeffrey Holland as Spike Dixon
Su Pollard as Peggy
David Griffin as Clive Dempster
Barry Howard as Barry Stuart Hargreaves

The series in set between 1959-60 in the Maplins holiday camp in the fictional town of Crimpton on sea in Essex, England.

A long running series about an old style British holiday camp in the 1950s. Based on real companies such as Butlins, the series is about the entertainers at the camp who are a series of struggling actors and entertainers and people who used to be famous. The series is set during a time when the British holiday camp was starting to change as people were going abroad for holidays.

There are a number of great characters in the series. Many of them have had their career go downhill and resent having to work at the holiday camp. Some of the younger entertainers are enthusiastic as they see the camp as a way to further their career.

Peggy a simple cleaner dreams of becoming a yellowcoat. Ted Bovis is bitter that he is not the head of the entertainments section - it has been given to the Cambridge educated Jeffrey Fairbrother who is unsuited for the post. Ted is always involved in a number of money making scams. Also the unseen head of the camp company is depicted as being mildly crooked. The series has a great catchphrase Hi De Hi! - a greeting at the camp. It is a great period piece with many well depicted characters.

I'm Alan Partridge

BBC

Written by Peter Baynham, Steve Coogan and Armando Iannucci

Two series of twelve episodes.

First show between 3 November 1997-16th December 2002.

Stars:

Steve Coogan as Alan Partridge
Felicity Montagu as Lynn Benfield
Simon Greenall as Michael
Phil Cornwell as Dave Clifton
Sally Phillips as Sophie
Barbara Durkin as Susan

Television and radio personality is down on his luck living in a cheap motorway hotel (a travel tavern). He is waiting for the BBC to renew his tv series and hosting a radio programme on local radio.

A classic television series starring Coogan's Alan Partridge character. Partridge had been played by Coogan in various guises on radio and television shows The Day Today (1994) and Knowing Me Knowing You (1994-95). These were spoof television programmes. This departure for the character is a rather surreal sitcom showing Partridge living in a hotel off a motorway waiting to get a new series from the BBC before buying a new house. The new setup worked very well with Alan's eccentric behaviour and interactions with the hotel staff and his desperate attempts to get his new tv series.

One good aspect is the scenes of Alan presenting his radio show - a format Coogan revisited in Mid Morning Matters. The first series has many classic - often bizarre – moments, such as Alan proposing a series of bizarre television show ideas and titles to a BBC executive. A second series was made where Alan was building a new house, living in a caravan on site with his Ukrainian girlfriend Sonja. This is also well regarded and has a selection of classic moments. But it is not quite as perfect as the hotel set series 1.

Just Good Friends

BBC

Written by John Sullivan

Twenty two episodes over three series.

First shown between 22nd September 1983 - 25th December 1986.

Stars:

Paul Nicholas as Vince Pinner
Jan Francis as Penny Warrender
John Ringham as Norman Warrender
Sylvia Kay as Daphne Warrender
Shaun Curry as Les Pinner
Ann Lynn as Rita Pinner
Adam French as Clifford Pinner

Vince Pinner and Penny Warrinder wedding was ruined after Vince jilted her at the alter. Five years later they meet in a pub. They decide to remain friends - but will their romance be rekindled.

A charming romance sitcom from John Sullivan. Vince Pinner is a more working class character who works as a bookmaker. His family have become rich scrap metal dealers. Penny comes from a more middle class background and works as a secretary for an advertising firm.

Nicholas and Francis are wonderful and funny in their roles and make the programme and have good chemistry. Writer John Sullivan wanted to create a good leading role for a woman and succeeded.

Vince's parents are played by Shaun Curry and Ann Lynn and are very good as the working class couple who have made a lot of money through their business. Penny's parents are John Ringham who plays a kind character and Sylvia Kay as the very funny snobbish and very sarcastic Daphne. One funny aspect of the show is how Daphne does not like Vince – calling him "thing".

There is a great ongoing romantic story over three episodes where we are left guessing whether the two will become lovers again.

A Christmas special before series three was a prequel showing how the pair met and their ill fated wedding. The series has an 80's atmosphere and a nice theme song sung by Nicholas.

Keeping Up Appearances

BBC

Written by Roy Clarke

Forty four episodes over five series.

First shown between 29th October 1990-25th December 1995.

Stars:

Patricia Routledge as Hyacinth Bucket
Clive Swift as Richard Bucket
Josephine Tewson as Elizabeth
Judy Cornwell as Daisy
Geoffrey Hughes as Onslow
Shirley Stelfox/Mary Millar as Rose
David Griffin as Emmet

Hyacinth Bucket comes from a lower class background and members of her lower class family live locally. But she sees herself as middle class and a respected middle class and refined member of the community. She pronounces Bucket Bouquet and is constantly trying to ingratiate herself with upper class people and lifestyles.

A classic comedy that could not be more English. Hyacinth is house proud and always trying to plan and attend events that would show off her middle class manners. Routledge gives an absolutely amazing performance as thr often crazed Hyacinth. Her physical and vocal comedy skills are fantastic. Hyacinth Bouquet is an iconic character and regarded as one of the best characters on British television. Clive Swift is wonderful as the long suffering wife of Hyacinth Richard with his amusing facial expressions. All the cast contribute to the series. Geoffrey Hughes has another classic character with Hyacinth's brother in law Onslow, a slob, idler and philosopher. At first glance the series seems awful with stock characters, repetitive jokes - the same jokes and scenes are used every week. But the repetition works of the jokes works and the section of comedy characters means the programme is hilarious. Each episode is rather like a wonderful English stage farce. The series looks great too with lots of outside locations.

The series was very popular at home and abroad. There could have been more series but Patricia Routledge did not want be too typecast as Hyacinth.

Last Of The Summer Wine

BBC

Written by Roy Clarke

Two hundred and ninety five episodes over thirty

one series.

First show between 4 January 1973 –29 August
2010

Stars:

Bill Owen as Compo Simmonite
Peter Sallis as Norman Clegg
Brian Wilde as Foggy Dewhurst
Kathy Staff as Nora Batty
Jane Freeman as Ivy
Frank Thornton as Truly Truelove
Michael Bates as Cyril Blamire
Michael Aldridge as Seymoor Utterhwaite

The series in set in small town west Yorkshire
and is about a group of elderly men and their
eccentric adventures.

A classic long running sitcom: it is the longest
running sitcom in the world which probably means
it should be in this book. The series started off
focusing on the trio of Compo, Clegg and Cyril.
Later the members of the trio changed – for
example Brian Wilde's foggy replaced Cyril as an
iconic part of the team. Deaths of cast members
meant a change of acting - main character in the
shoe Compo was changed after Bill Owen's death
in 1999. Pete Sallis was a mainstay of the series.
Later the series became an ensemble piece with
extensive use of outside locations in the Yorkshire
moors. Veteran British comedy actors such as
Bert Kwok, Brian Murphy and June Whitfield were

brought in.

The series had gentle humour and was slow paced. Stock characters such as henpecked husbands and dominant wives obsessed with housework were prominent. In many ways it was about ageing with the older men almost becoming children again and taking part in bizarre schemes and adventures which often involved Compo such as putting him a rocket. A popular well written show with some dramatic pieces along with the humour.

The League Of Gentlemen

BBC

Written by Jeremy Dyson, Mark Gatiss, Steve Pemberton and Reece Shearsmith

Twenty two episodes over three series.

First shown between 11th January to 20th December 2017.

Stars:

Mark Gatiss
Steve Pemberton
Reece Shearsmith

as various characters.

Royston Vasey is a town in the north of England. It is home to some bizarre people and strange things often occur there.

A classic comedy horror series staring Mark Gatiss, Steve Pemberton and Reece Shearsmith. Jeremy Dyson the fourth member of the group who only writes the series. Gatiss, Pemberton and Shearsmith play numerous strange characters. The characters are very memorable and over the top. They include two extremely odd people who run a small remote shop, a very strange couple obsessed with toads and hygiene hosting their nephew, a strange butcher selling an illegal meat item in demand, an unemployment centre worker who hates unemployed people, an old 1970s rocker trying to reform his group...

There are horror influenced storylines with lashings of dark humour. The show is very surreal and the creators are big horror aficionados which can be seen in the series. The series started off as a radio programme. One fantastic episode is the 2000 extended Christmas special. It is made in the style of a British 1970's anthology horror film with three different tales. A film was made in 2005 called The League of Gentlemen's Apocalypse which was well received.

Shearsmith and Pemberton made another similar series Psychoville. This ran for two series and fourteen episodes between 2009-2011. The two actors again played different characters in a horror themed storyline.

Man About the House

ITV

Written by Brian Cooke and Johnnie Mortimer

Thirty nice episodes over six series.

Stars:

Richard O' Sullivan as Robin Tripp
Paula Wilcox as Chrissy Plummer
Sally Thosett as Jo
Yootha Joyce as Mildred Roper
Brian Murphy as George Roper
Doug Fisher as Larry Simmonds

Women Chrissy and Jo live in a London flat in a building owned by the Ropers. They take on student chef Robin Tripp on as a flatmate.

A pleasant seventies sitcom with a great cast. Robin O'Sullivan is very good as Robin Tripp giving his usual charming performance. The two "girls" Paula Wilcox and Sally Thomsett are very funny. Yootha Joyce and Brian Murphy worked so well together and in the series that they were given their own spin-off sitcom - George and Mildred. The show is very colourful entertaining comedy with good plots and scripts. What more can one ask from a seventies British sitcom? A memorable theme tune completes the package.

The series has a great theme tune - Up to Date by Johnny Hawkesworth. A film version was made in 1974 which is a fun adaption. As well as George and Mildred, Robin Tripp has his own spin off Robin's Nest. This ran for forty eight episodes over six series from 1977-81. In the series Robin runs a bistro with his girlfriend Vicky played by Tessa Wyatt. Vicky's father played by Tony Britton owns the building the restaurant it is in. Irish actor David Kelly has a memorable role as a one armed Irish restaurant assistant!

Mr. Bean

ITV

Written by Rowan Atkinson, Robin Driscoll, Ben Elton and Richard Curtis.

Fifteen episodes.

First shown between 1st January 1990-15th December 1995.

Stars:

Rowan Atkinson as Mr Bean

Mr Bean is an eccentric childish character who uses strange solutions for everyday problems.

An extremely popular programme throughout the

world, Rowan Atkinson's Mr Bean character is according to Atkinson a "child in a man's body". The programme has little dialogue and is like a modern version of silent comedy shorts of the 1920s or the work of Jacques Tati, and relies on Atkinson's physical comedy with his facial expressions and actions.

Mr Bean has a series of iconic items such as his tweed jacket, teddy and lime green mini car. Mr Bean can be quite nasty to other people too, which provides humour.

It is said that Mr Bean finds bizarre solutions to everyday problems, which again provides the comedy. The 14 short episodes (plus a compilation episode) with their English setting work very well and are classic pieces of television.

Two feature films have been made. Bean in 1997 which sees Bean go to Los Angeles. And Mr Bean's Holiday 2007 which sees Bean travel through France. The films are ok but not as charming as the more compact tv series.

Never the Twain

ITV

Written by Johnnie Mortimer

Sixty seven episodes over eleven series.

First shown between 7th September 1981 - 8th October 1991.

Stars:

Windsor Davies as Oliver Smallbridge
Donald Sinden as Simon Peel
Derek Deadman as Ringo
Teddy Turner as Banks

Oliver Smallbridge and Windsor Davies are rival antique dealers with shops next to each other. They are also next door neighbours. They used to be business partners but had a bitter fall out. They are always trying to get one over on the other. To complicate matters Smallbridge's daughter and Peel's son are in love and plan to marry.

A surprisingly long running British sitcom but an extremely fun one elevated by the charm of its stars. Windsor Davies and Donald Sinden are a delight trying to out ham each other in every scene. Their attempts to get one over on the other and their various insults are very funny. There is a good ensemble cast with Derek Deadman as Smallbridge's buffoonish shop assistant Ringo, and Peel's butler Banks.

Some great plots and a memorable theme tune all add to a charming 80s British comedy.

The New Statesman

ITV

Written by Laurence Marks and Maurice Gran

Four series of twenty-six episodes.

First shown between 13th September 1987 – 30th December 1994.

Stars:

Rik Mayall as Alan B'Stard
Michael TroughtonSir Piers Fletcher-Dervish
Marsha FitzalanSarah B'Stard

Alan B'Stard is a right wing British Conservative MP. He is dishonest and scheming and has a rather colourful private life.

The series is a great satire on the Thatcherite political era of the 1980s. Alan is a very good vehicle for the comedy of Rik Mayall. The typically charismatic Mayall creates a memorable, iconic character as the amoral right-wing conservative MP which was a great satire on real life politicians. There are some great, fun plots in the series with Alan's outlandish schemes, pursuit of extreme free market economics (such as scrapping state pensions) and debauched behaviour often mirroring real life scandals.

One good thing about the series was that the fourth series had Alan becoming a member of the European Parliament which allowed for European themed plots and satire of the European Union. The series is wonderfully produced and has a very good ensemble cast.

The Office

BBC

Written by Ricky Gervais and Stephen Merchant

Fourteen episodes over two series.

First shown between 9 July 2001 – 27 December 2003.

Stars:

Ricky Gervais as David Brent
Martin Freeman as Tim Canterbury
Mackenzie Crook as Gareth Keenan
Lucy Davis as Dawn Tinsley

David Brent is the general manager at the Wernham Hogg paper company based on the Slough Trading Estate in England.

A classic mockumentary by the inimitable Ricky Gervais.

The series is quite short - trying to copy short lived classic such as Fawlty Towers. The series depicts the mundane world of English office life with typically dull and mildly eccentric characters. Brent is a classic creation desperately trying to be humorous and making gaffes and social faux pas. There are a range of other great characters such as nerdy jobsworth Gareth, pleasant everyman Tim, and the eccentric Keith with his strange slowly spoken dialogue. The series is short and has a good plot with storylines involving Brent's position and romantic subplots. As everyone knows now Gervais's writing is very sharp and often politically incorrect at times, but very funny. Also included are dramatic and quite moving scenes. There are many classic lines and scenes.

A popular US version was made. It ran for two hundred and one episodes over nine series from March 24th 2005-May 16th 2013.

A film version was made in 2016 - David Brent: Life on the Road. Only Brent appears from the characters in the tv series.

The Old Guys

BBC

Written by Jesse Armstrong and Sam Bain

Twelve episodes over two series.

Stars:

Roger Lloyd-Pack as Tom
Clive Swift as Roy
Jane Asher as Sally
Katherine Parkinson as Amber

Retired Tom and Roy share a house - which is Roy's. Sally moves in over the street, and Tom and Rou both find her attractive.

An underrated modern sitcom staring legendary actors from other sitcoms Roger Lloyd-Pack and Clive Swift. They give great performances as you would expect. The characters are very fun with the slightly odd Tom and pompous Roy.

There are some great plots and many funny lines. The series is slightly offbeat, almost quirky. The humour is very British. It is a shame that more episodes were not made.

One Foot in the Grave

BBC

Written by David Renwick

Six series of forty-two episodes

First shown from 4 January 1990 –20 November 2000

Stars:

Richard Wilson as Victor Meldrew
Annette Crosbie as Margaret Meldrew
Doreen Mantle as Jean Warboys
Angus Deayton as Patrick Trench
Janine Duvitski as Pippa Trench
Owen Brenman as Nick Swainey

Victor Meldrew has been mad redundant from his job as a security guard aged 60 and been replaced by an answering machine,. Victor tries to find work and occupy himself, being driven mad bu the behaviour of the general public and often driving his wife Margaret insane in the process.

A classic sitcom from David Renwick. Richard Wilson plays his iconic Victor Meldrew character, a man driven to extreme grumpiness by the annoyances of the modern world, such as yobbish behaviour and annoying tradesmen.

As well as a wonderful performance by Richard Wilson as Victor, there is a great ensemble cast with Annette Crosbie with a very interesting character as Victor's wife Margaret; the very funny Doreen Mantle as Jean who is always insulting everyone without realising it and a great addition to many episodes; Angus Deayton and Janine Duvitski as the couple's neighbours - Patrick has a feud with victor; and Owen Brenman as the eccentric neighbour Nick Swainey who is always coming out with bizarre phrases.

Victor often ends up in a bizarre and embarrassing
situations through no fault of his own - and as a
result he is considered mad by neighbours and
others.

Although the series relies on slapstick and farce
there is depth to the humour which is quite dark
at times. Also we get a lot of depth to Victor and
Margaret's characters with their discussion of their
life. The series was quite long running with many
classic episodes and moments. There was often a
special episode in each series which took place in
one setting (technically called a bottle episode").

There were seven Christmas specials including a
feature length episode One Foot in the Algarve.
The series had a special final episode which is
rather good too. And who can forget Victor's
famous catchphrase:"I don't believe it".

British comedian Les Dawson was one person
considered for the part of Victor.

Only Fools And Horses

BBC

Written by John Sullivan

Sixty four episodes over seven series.

First shown from 8 September 1981 –25

December 2003

Stars:

David Jason as Del Boy Trotter
Nicholas Lyndhurst as Rodney Trotter
Lennard Pearce as Grandad Trotter
Buster Merryfield as Uncle Albert
Gwyneth Strong as Cassandra
Tessa Peake-Jones as Raquel
John Challis as Boycie
Roger Loyd Pack as Trigger
Paul Barber as Denzil

Del Boy Trotter lives with his younger brother Rodney and Grandfather in a lower class tower block in Peckham in London. Del Boy is a market trader often selling illegal goods - such as stolen electrical items. Del Boy dreams of being a rich entrepreneur and engages in many get rich quick schemes.

An iconic series that had a great impression in British popular culture and was extremely popular when shown. the episode Time on Our Hands shown on December 26th 1996 holds the record for viewers for a sitcom in Britain with 24 million watching.

Del Boy is a great character played wonderfully by David Jason. He is famous for his malapropisms - often involving foreign languages, garish dress sense, and his use of insults such as plonker and dipstick. There is a great cast of characters with the daft Trigger played by Roger Lloyd Pack, car dealer Boycie with his distinctive laugh and many other locals who appear during the series. Of course Nicholas Lyndhurst shares top billing with Jason as Rodney and is wonderful during the series. The programme started off as a regular half an hour sitcom.

Series six was made up of extended episodes of 50 minutes. The format of extended specials continued until 1996's trilogy of episodes shown at Christmas which was intended to be the end of the series. But five years later the series was brought back for three more specials (which in my opinion did not work too well).

Lennard Pearce died at the end of season 4. He was replaced by Buster Merryfield as the Trotter's Uncle Albert and became a good character for the series. Only Fools had many iconic episodes and memorable comedy moments, along with some great dramatic moments which were not out of place. Writer John Sullivan created such as good selection of characters and settings that it must have been easy to write!

On the Buses

ITV

Written by Ronald Chesney and Ronald Wolfe

Seventy four episodes over seven series.

First shown between 28 February 1969 –20 May 1973

Stars:

Reg Varney as Stan Butler
Bob Grant as Jack Harper
Anna Karen as Olive Rudge
Doris Hare as Cicely CourtneidgeMabel "Mum" Butler
Stephen Lewis as Inspector Cyril "Blakey" Blake
Michael Robbins as Arthur Rudge

Stan Butler lives with his mother, sister Olive and Olive's husband Arthur. He works for the Luxton bus Company as a driver. There he works with conductor Jack and Inspector Blake.

A popular and famous sitcom. It is unpretentious and seems at first glance to be poorly made with weak storylines and characters. But it is a wonderful traditional British sitcom with memorable characters and great plotlines.

The cast are superb with Varney giving a good comic and dramatic performance. Grant is brilliant as the lecherous Jack. Hare and Robbins are good comic actors and are good in their working class roles with Arthur a wonderful pompous character with a sarcastic turn of phrase. Stephen Lewis creates a classic comedy character with his officious bus inspector and catchphrase "get that bus out". The plots are great fun and the series in very colourful (even if the first two series were in black and white). The series is actually an interesting depiction of working class life and has some dramatic moments. It is almost influenced by the 60s British kitchen sink school of drama. Some have said it is sexist with the older Jack and Stan chasing after young women - but most of the time the younger women make them look foolish.

The series was so popular that three films were made: On the Buses (1971), Mutiny on the Buses (1972), and Holiday on the Buses (1973). A spin featuring Blakey was made. Don't Drink The Water Ran for thirteen episodes over two series between 1974–75. The strange plot had Blakey retire to an apartment block in Spain with his sister. It's a strange setting, but good fun due to the strength of the Blakey character.

Open All Hours

BBC

Written by Roy Clarke

Twenty six episodes over four series

First shown between 23 March 1973 – 6 October 1985

Stars:

Ronnie Barker as Arkwright
David Jason as Granville
Lynda Baron as Nurse Gladys Emmanuel

Arkwright runs a small old fashioned grocer's shop in Doncaster in Yorkshire. He is assisted by his nephew Granville.

A charming sitcom. Barker plays tight fisted stuttering Arkwright always looking to avoid spending money and trying to rip off his customers.

Jason plays the young Granville who has romantic dreams of a more exiting life and a nice girlfriend. Arkwright is romantically involved with Nurse Gladys Emmanuel and there are a selection of regular often eccentric customers.

One particularly nice part of the series is at the end where Arkwright is shown getting stuff in from outside the shop at closing time accompanied by a voice-over of Arkwright's views on the day. One aspect of the programme is that Arkwright has a stutter which is used for comic purposes.

The series started off as a pilot in a series of Ronnie Barker comedy episodes Seven of One in 1973. Series on followed in 1976, then there was a gap before series 2 in 1981.

Still Open All Hours is a revived version of the show. Forty one episodes have been made over six series from 23rd December 2013. In this new version Granville has taken over the shop which looks very similar to the one in the original series. The joke is that Granville has almost turned into Arkwright. It is quite popular - six series have been made. But as a fan of the original it does not seem quite right that the Granville character would have morphed into Arkwright.

Phoenix Nights

Channel 4

Written by Peter Kay, Dave Spikey, Peter Fitzmaurice

Two series of twelve episodes.

First shown between 14 November 2001- 12 September 2002

Stars:

Peter Kay as Brian Potter/Max/various
Dave Spikey as Jerry St Clair
Justin Moorhouse as Young Kenny
Paddy McGuiness as Paddy

Wheelchair bound Brian Potter runs a traditional working men's club in Bolton in the north of England.

A wonderful unique show from modern day comedy legend. The show is set in a downmarket working class club found in the north of England. The club has variety acts and other entertainments. The awfulness of many of these acts provides much humour. Kay is a delight as the mean and sarcastic Potter. There are numerous other great characters too all funny in a northern English style. Only twelve episodes were made but the series is very funny, stylishly made and has great plots.

Another recent highly regarded Kay sitcom is Car Share. In this Peter Kay plays a supermarket worker who share a car with a female worker to work. This ran from 2015-2020 for twelve episodes over three series.

Porridge

BBC

Written by Dick Clement and Ian La Frenais

Twenty one episodes over three series.

First shown between 1 April 1973-25 March 1977.

Stars:

Ronnie Barker as Norman Stanley Fletcher
Fulton Mackay as Principal officer Mr MacKay

Richard Beckinsale as Lennie Godber
Brian Wilde as Prison officer Mr Henry
Barrowclough
Peter Vaughan as "Genial" Harry Grout
Sam Kelly as "Bunny" Warren
Tony Osoba as Jim McLaren
Michael Barrington as Geoffrey Venables (the
Governor)
Christopher Biggins as Lukewarm
David Jason as Blanco

Londoner Norman Stanley Fletcher is serving time
in a northern English prison. Fletcher's cellmate is
a young man called Lennie Godber who is in
prison for the first time. The older Fletcher takes
Godber under his wing and helps him to survive
prison.
A classic comedy with legendary character actor
Ronnie Barker absolutely fantastic as Norman
Fletcher. The programme gives a look into the
problems prisoners face and life in prison. The
viewer has sympathy for characters such as
Fletcher and Godber as they deal with prison life
and discuss why they are in prison. Although life
in the prison does not look that appetising, the
series is still a sitcom with humorous plots and the
darker side of prison life is sanitised. The prison in
the series (the fictional HMP Slade) is a category
C prison: A is a Maximum security prison and D is
an open prison.

As well as Barker giving an exemplary character
acting performance, there is a good cast of
characters such as Fulton Mackay as the harsh

prison officer Mackay and Brian Wilde as the more sympathetic and progressive officer Barrowclough. Fletcher is often battling with Mackay and trying to gain small victories over him. The series was popular with prisoners. a prisoner wrote in a newspaper article:

"the conflict between Fletcher and Officer Mackay was about the most authentic depiction ever of the true relationship that exists between prisoners and prison officers in British jails up and down the country. I'm not sure how, but writers Dick Clement and Ian La Frenais ... grasped the notion that it is the minor victories against the naturally oppressive prison system that makes prison life bearable".

One interesting piece of casting was David Jason as elderly prisoner Blanco. For Porridge Barker of course played a younger man and died his hair brown. In Open All Hours Barker plays the older shopkeeper Arkwright with Jason as his younger nephew.
Various real prisons were used for exterior and other scenes, and a special Ealing studios set was used for some exterior shots. This gives the series an authentic look.

Ronnie Barker stopped making Porridge as he did not want to keep playing the same character. But, a sequel was made Going Straight which depicted Fletcher released from prison and at home. This only ran for one series. In 1978. It was decided to end the series after Richard Beckinsdale died in

1979.

A very good and popular film version was made in 1979. Beckinsale died just before the film was released.

Red Dwarf

BBC/Dave

Written by Rob Grant and Doug Naylor

Seventy four episodes over twelve series.

First shown from 15 February 1988 – present

Stars:

Craig Charles as David "Dave" Lister
Chris Barrie as Arnold Judas Rimmer:
Danny John-Jules as the Cat:
Robert Llewellyn as Kryten 2X4B-523P:
Norman Lovett and Hattie Hayridge as Holly:

In the late 21st century the mining ship Red Dwarf has a radiation leak which kills everyone on board apart from Dave Lister who was in stasis. The ships computer keeps Lister in stasis for 3 million years until radiation returns to normal. Lister is now the last human in the universe. He is joined on board by a human like person who has evolved from Lister's cat and a hologram of

Lister's crewmate Rimmer.

A cult sci-fi sitcom. The set up of the characters on a huge spaceship in outer space allows for some wonderful plots - often involving science fiction. It is rather like Star Trek with the crew meeting different aliens or encountering strange phenomena every episode. Lister and Rimmer are great characters who, in a familiar sitcom plot, dislike each other as they are different types of characters. Lister is slovenly. Rimmer is tidy and keen to better himself - but can't as he is incompetent. Kryton the android was a great addition in series three.

The classic era of the series was with the first six series. With series 7 and 8 only Doug Naylor was the writer and there was a change in tone and storylines.

After series seven in 1999 on the BBC the show was revived in 2009 on Dave for three series and a few specials. The revival rebooted the series to just have the original main characters on Red Dwarf.

There were many great episodes and great lines and scenes. The show remains very popular today.

Rising Damp

BBC

Written by Eric Chappell

Twenty eight episodes over four series.

First shown from 2 September 1974-9 May 1978.

Stars:

Leonard Rossiter as Rigsby
Frances de la Tour as Miss Jones
Richard Beckinsale as Alan
Don Warrington as Philip Smith

Rigsby is the owner of a dilapidated building in Leeds England. He rents out rooms to various people.

A great vehicle for the comic acting of Leonard Rossiter. There are four interesting main characters in the series. Rigsby as the shabby, tight fisted landlord. Alan is a medical student. Rigsby is often a father figure to Alan. Philip is a black student who shares a room with Alan. Rigsby is fascinated by Philip who states he is an African Prince. The narrow minded and often racist Rigbsy is very interested in Alan's life and his success with women. Miss Jones is a lonely, romantic woman who Rigsby admires and wants to have a relationship with.

Rigsby mostly argues with other characters but they get to know each other and help each other at times.

The series is stagey and studio based. The series was adapted from a stage play written by Eric Chappel titled The Banana Box which featured all the main cast apart from Beckensdale. The show has elements of a stage farce. The cast is made up of a group of talented actors and all give great performances. Rossiter is good as the fidgety Rigsby; Rossiter delivery and comic timing is superb. Rigsby has a famous catchphrase "Miss Jones" delivered often in a high pitched way.

There are a number of good plots, often involving other tenants in the house. One recurring theme is Rigsby trying to social climb and being obsequious to every member of a higher class he meets - who often then rebuff him. Rigsby is a Conservative, the others supporters of the left wing Labour.

A film was made in 1980 combining several plots from the series and stage play. Sadly Richard Beckinsdale died in 1979 and he was replaced by Christopher Strauli in the film.

The series is regarded as one of commercial station ITV's best sitcoms.

The Royle Family

BBC

Written by Caroline Ahern, Craig Cash, Phil Mealey

Twenty five episodes over three series.

First shown between 14September 1998-25 December 2012.

Stars:
Ricky Tomlinson as Jim Royale
Sue Johnston as Barbara Royale
Caroline Ahern as Denise Royal/Best
Craig Cash as Dave Best
Ralf Little as Antony Royale
Liz Smith as Nana
Geoffrey Hughes as Twiggy
Jessica Hynes as Cheryl

Working class couple Jim and Barbara Royale live in Manchester with son Antony. Daughter Denise is engaged to Dave.

A classic, charming comedy from Caroline Ahern and Craig Cash. The series takes place in the Royale's house, and in particular their living room. The characters are invariably watching tv and talking.

As well as the Royales, other characters visit such as next door neighbours Joe and Doreen Caroll and their daughter Cheryl, and their criminal friend Twiggy.

Like several other British sitcoms such as Only Fools and Horses, the series originally ran for three series of six episodes over thirty minutes. Several years later it was brought back for a series of irregular extended specials, mostly shown on Christmas Day, which hard large viewing figures.

The series has some dramatic elements and no laugh track. But it is very funny due to the humour of the writers Caroline Ahern and Craig Cash who write many funny dialogues about mundane, everyday subjects for the characters.

Shelley

ITV

First shown between 12July 1979-1 September 1992.

Written by Peter Tilbury, Andy Hamilton and Guy Jenkin, Colin Bostock-Smith, David Frith, Bernard McKenna and Barry Pilton.

Seventy one episodes over ten series.

Stars:

Hywel Bennett as James Shelley
Belinda Sinclair as Francis Shelley
Warren Clarke as Paul England

28 years old James Shelley has a doctorate in Geography but is often unemployed and refusing to work. He is sardonic and anti-establishment.

An entertaining series with a wonderful character in Shelley, the intelligent man with a philosophical outlook on society and a very sarcastic sense of humour. The series has great writing and Hywel Bennett is a good piece of casting for Shelley and his dry sense of humour; he has good comic timing The series often has Shelley mocking cultural fashions of the time such as the Yuppie. There are a range of interesting scripts and characters for Shelley to muse about life to or rail against.

The series lasted for twelve years and there were many episodes. The writers changed so naturally there are changes in style and quality during the series, but it remains a wonderful slightly different sitcom with a classic central character.

Series 7 was made in 1988 four years after series 6. It was entitled the Return of Shelley. Shelley had returned from teaching English in the middle east.

Sorry!

BBC

Written by Ian Davidson and Peter Vincent

Forty two episodes over seven series.

First shown between 12 March 1981-10 October 1988

Stars:

Ronnie Corbett as Timothy Lumsden
Barbara Lott as Phyllis Lumsden
William Moore as Sidney Lumsden
Marguerite Hardiman as Muriel
Derek Fuke as Kevin
Roy Holder as Frank Baker

Librarian Timothy Lumsden lives at home with his father and dominant mother. Timothy wants to leave home but his mother keeps him there.

A fun, slightly strange comedy with British comedy legend Ronnie Corbett. It was a long running show and Corbett is wonderful with his charm and natural comic timing and persona. A great comic character is created with Phyllis Lumsden and her eccentric behaviour – she is like a character from a Harold Pinter play. Those of a certain age will remember Timothy's father catchphrase "language Timothy", stated when

Timothy is not even saying anything bad. The series is slightly offbeat and almost surreal and there are numerous interesting often fantasy based plot lines in the series.

A charming comedy with some dark humour that was very popular when first shown. And it also has a classic theme tune.

Steptoe And Son

BBC

Written by Ray Galton and Alan Simpson

Fifty Seven episodes over eight series.

First shown from 7 June 1962 –26 December 1974

Stars:

Harry H Corbett as Harold Steptoe
Wilfred Brambell as Albert Steptoe

Rag and bone man Albert lives in Shepherd's Bush in London with his son Harold who works as the rag and bone man.

A classic television series. Brambell and Corbett are extremely good as their characters which have great depth. There is a sense of social realism in the show and good working class dialogue and a funny use of slang expertly delivered by the actors. Harold wants to better himself and move on but he is trapped with his father and his attempts to better himself often go wrong because of his failings or those from higher classes stopping him - or his father ruining it. For example Harold will take up a new hobby and Albert will end up being an expert in it. The series has an element of drama along with the comedy with its depiction of the working class pair and their life.

Of course mostly the humour and situations are often unrealistic and over the top for comedic purposes. There were many classic moments in the series, including an episode where the feuding pair divided up the house!

Two films were made in the 1970s: Steptoe and Son (1972) and Steptoe and Son Ride Again (1973).

There are two classic Christmas specials too. Even though the BBC often wiped tapes of programmes in the 60s/70s all episodes survive; although all the first colour series and all but two of the second colour series in the 70s only exist in black and white.

Still Game

BBC

Written by Ford Kiernan and Greg Hemphill

Sixty two episodes over nine series.

First shown from 6 September 2002-28 March 2019.

Stars:

Ford Kiernan as Jack Jarvis Esq.
Greg Hemphill as Victor McDade
Paul Riley as Winston Ingram
Mark Cox as Thomas "Tam" Mullen
Jane McCarry as Isa Drennan
Sanjeev Kohli as Navid Harrid
Gavin Mitchell as Robert "Boabby The Barman" Taylor

Jack Jarvis Esq and Victor McDade are two pensioners living in a flat in a working class Glasgow who ruminate on the changes to the city.

A classic Scottish cult comedy. The two main characters, the actors are made up to look older, are great characters giving their views on modern society, reminiscing and refusing to lead he life of a pensioner.

Kiernan and Hempill both wrote for various cult

Scottish sketch shows and this is reflected in the numerous number of wonderful characters in Still Game. There are interesting plots revolving around life in working class Glasgow, lots of greats, lines, dark humour and some drama. A very popular show, particularly in Scotland.

It is one of those typically Scottish comedies that for some reason were only shown in Scotland to begin with. From the fourth series it was also shown in the rest of Britain.

Terry and June

BBC

Written by John Kane

Sixty five episodes over nine series.

First shown from 24 October 1979-31 August 1987.

Stars:

June Whitfield as June Medford
Terry Scott as Terry Medford
Reginald Marsh as Sir Dennis Hodge
Terence Alexander – Malcolm Harris (series 1 and 2)
Tim Barrett – Malcolm Harris (1980 Special to series 7)

John Quayle – Malcolm Harris (series 8 and 9)
Rosemary Frankau – Beattie Harris

Terry and June Medford live a comfortable middle class suburban existence in Purley in London. Terry has to deal with his often eccentric boss Sir Dennis Hodge at the fire extinguisher business he works at.

Terry and June was a very popular sitcom. It was a remake of the seventies sitcom Happy Ever After which also starred Scott and Whitfield. The series was often lampooned as being a typical cosy sitcom where the main male character works in an office and comes home to his rather large house to drink whisky from a decanter while his wife stays at home. But the thing about Terry and June is that it is funny and entertaining, and is a wonderful comedy in the vein of British farces. Whitfield and Scott are legendary comic actors and make the show. Reginald Marsh is brilliant as Sir Dennis who is almost a parody of the sitcom office boss. In fact the whole show seems like a parody of the traditional British sitcom about a middle class businessman married to a housewife living in a large suburban house.

There are many classic episodes. Memorable episodes include the Christmas specials, one where they look after a country pub and an episode where they take a day trip to Boulogne in France. One fantastic part of the series is the opening credits depicting the Medford's having drinks in their garden; every time a different thing

happens such as the chair collapsing! All
accompanied by an iconic jaunty theme.

Till Death Us Do Part

BBC

Written by Johnny Speight

Fifty four episodes over seven series.

First shown from 6 June 1966-16 December 1975.

Stars:

Warren Mitchell as Alf Garnett
Dandy Nichols as Elsie Garnett
Una Stubbs as Rita
Anthony Booth as Mike

In the East End of London working class
conservative Alf Garnett lives with his wife Elsie,
daughter Rita and socialist son in law Mike.

An iconic series which sees working class and
racist Alf Garnett lock horns with his socially
liberal and socialist son in law Mike. The series
dealt with issues in Britain at the time such as
racism, immigration and increasingly liberal social
attitudes. Alf was intended by writer Johnny
Speight to be mocked for his racism. Although the
racist language and depictions mean that the

show is not repeated now on British television. Many episodes have Alf and his family discussing the issues of the day. The series is a landmark one and the characters are amusing. There are great performances from the principle cast members.

16 episodes are missing.

Two films were made - Till Death Us Do Part (1969), a pleasant look at the Garnett's from World War 2 to the present day which is an interesting look at Britain in the period. And The Alf Garnett Saga (1972) which was less well received and rarely shown on British tv.

Alf Garnett was a popular character who made numerous appearances on British television.

A series called Till Death was made in 1980 where the Garnet's move to the coast at Eastbourne. Six episodes were made. Alf returned for ~I Sickness and i Health which ran between 1st September 1985-3rd April 1992. Forty seven episodes over six series were made. This was a very good series with a good ensemble cast and more sanitised than Till Death to Us Part.

The Archie Bunker character from American sitcom All in the Family was based on Alf Garnett.

To the Manor Born

BBC

Written by Peter Spence

Twenty episodes over three series.

First shown between 30 September 1979-29 November 1981.

Stars:

Penelope Keith as Audrey fforbes-Hamilton
Peter Bowles as Richard de Vere
Angela Thorne as Marjory Frobisher
Daphne Heard as Mrs. Maria Polouvicka (Mrs. Poo)
John Rudling as Brabinger (the Butler)
Michael Bilton as Old Ned
Gerald Sim as The Rector
Daphne Oxenford as Mrs. Patterson

In the fictional town of Grantleigh in Somerset, England Audrey fforbes-Hamilton sees her family estate (which has been owned for 400 years) sold after her recently deceased husband was declared bankrupt. She tries to buy the estate back at auction but is outbid by self-made millionaire Richard de Vere. Audrey moves into a house next to the estate with her butler.

A charming British sitcom. It was intended as a vehicle for Penelope Keith after her success with

The Good Life. The comedy comes from Audrey being moved from her families estate by a Czech man who has made his fortune from owning supermarkets. Audrey and Richard are rivals in community activities, but they grow closer as rivals often do in television programmes before the viewer wonders whether they will become romantically involved. There is a great selection of characters in the country setting. Great plots are created in the English county setting. Of course Penelope Keith and Peter Bowles are wonderful and have a great chemistry. The series was very popular gaining huge audiences when first shown.

A 2007 special was shown on Christmas Day which caught up with Richard and Audrey in the present day.

Up Pompeii!

BBC

Written by Talbot Rothwell and Sid Colin

Thirteen episodes over two series. Plus a pilot and two specials

First shown between 1969-1975.

Stars:

Frankie Howard as Lurcio

Elizabeth Larner as Ammonia
Kerry Gardner as Nausius
Jeanne Mockford as Senna the Soothsayer
Wallas Eaton as Sen. Ludicrus Sextus
Max Adrian as Sen. Ludicrus Sextus
Georgina Moon as Erotica

In ancient Roman Pompeii slave Lurcio works for his master Luducrus Sectus and family.

A classic vehicle for the comedy of Frankie Howerd. He breaks through the fourth wall to talk to the audience and has an almost endless collection of double entendres and innuendo. Other Howerd staples such as complaining about the script and the other actors are here too. The series is great fun with a good setting. The plots are very good with elements of farce and slapstick. Carry On writer Talbot Rothwell wrote the scripts so that is both a sign that they will be entertaining and of the type of show Up Pompeii is.

Howerd returned for a special edition in 1991 entitled Further Up Pompeii.

A film Up Pompeii was made in 1971. Two variations of Up Pompeii with Howerd playing a similar character. Up the Chastity Belt (1971) was set in England in the 1100's. Up the Front (1972) is set during World War 1. Two tv series had a similar character and style. 1973's Whoops Baghdad set in medieval Iraq and 1982's Then Churchill Said to Me set during World War 2. Both ran for 6 episodes.

Whatever Happened to the Likely Lads?

BBC

Written by Dick Clement and Ian La Frenais

First shown from 9th January 1973-24th
December 1974.
Twenty-seven episodes over two series.

Stars:

James Bolam as Terry Collier
Rodney Bewes as Bob Ferris
Brigit Forsyth as Thelma Chambers
Shelia Fearn as Audrey

Childhood friends Bob Ferris and Terry Collier are
reunited in Newcastle after Terry leaves the army.
Bob is wanting to better his life and become
middle class by marrying Thelma, buying a house
and mixing in middle class social circles. The work
shy Terry has resumed his working class lifestyle.

A great sequel to The Likely Lads. The Likely Lads
ran for three series between 1964-1966 and
depicted Terry and Bob as young working class
men working in the same factory. At the end of
the Likely Lads Terry joins the army. Whatever
Happened to the Likely Lads? picks up the story

with Terry leaving the army to find Bob has become more middle class.

This is a wonderful charming series showing the social and building changes in Newcastle and in the characters life. Bob is trying to move away from his working class youth to become middle class and responsible marrying Thelma, buying a house and working for his father in laws firm. Terry still want to enjoy the party lifestyle of his youth and drags Bob into his world - which provides much of the plots and humour. The series has great use of locations and a wonderful theme. There are many classic episodes and moments. One episode where Bob and Terry are trying to avoid the result of an England football match so they can watch the highlights later is particularly memorable.

A very pleasant and watchable film was made in 1976 - The Likely Lads. Bolam and Bewes fell out during the making of the film which was a shame as it meant no more Likely Lads. Some more Likely Lads episodes, for example set in the 80s, would have been fun.

Yes Minister and Yes, Prime Minister

BBC

Written by Antony Jay and Jonathan Lynn

Twenty two episodes over three series of Yes Minster and sixteen episodes over two series of Yes Prime Minister.

First shown from 25th February 1980-28th January 1988.

Stars:

Paul Eddington as Jim Hacker
Nigel Hawthorne as Sir Humphrey Appleby
Derek Fowlds as Bernard Woolley

Jim Hacker is a British government minister in the Department of Administrative Affairs. He comes up against members of the civil service in the guise of Permanent Secretary Sir Humphrey Appleby, and Private Secretary Bernard Woolley. Later Hacker unexpectedly becomes Prime Minister again dealing with the two civil servants.

A classic political satire on the workings of British government. There are a number of great storylines which mimic real life battles between ministers and civil service officials inside government. The jokes and conundrums faced by Hacker and the civil servants are universal and faced by politicians today. No scenes were set in the British parliament as the writers stated the real work of politics is behind the scenes. British Prime Minister Margaret Thatcher was a fan. A wonderfully produced programme with great acting by the principle trio.

The Young Ones

BBC

Written by Ben Elton, Rik Mayall and Lise Mayer. Additional material: Alexei Sayle

Two series, twenty episodes in total.

First shown between 9 November 1982 –19 June 1984

Stars:

Adrian Edmondson as Vyvyan "Vyv" Basterd
Rik Mayall as Rick
Nigel Planer as Neil Pye
Christopher Ryan as Mike "The-Cool-Person",
Alexei Sayle as students' landlord Jerzei/various

Four university students from differing backgrounds share a house. They are hippy Neil, punk Vyvyan, the relatively normal but crooked Mike and anarchist Rick.

A classic and cult series from prominent alternative comedians of the early 80s. The sitcom genre is played around with and the series includes musical numbers, guest stars, talking puppets, cutaways, the breaking of the fourth wall etc. There is slapstick and surreal humour. The plots and dialogue often satirize political, cultural and social events at the time.

Edmondson and Mayall play characters they would play elsewhere as a double act, such as as the Dangerous Brothers and as Richard and Eddie in Bottom. Edmondson is memorable as the punk Vyvyan, and Mayall gives a usual mad, charismatic performance as the anarchist student Rick. Nigel Planer is great as always as hippy Neil. Christopher Ryan gives a typically interesting performance as Mike the leader of the group,

Another show with a similar cast was made called Filthy Rich and Catflap. Six episodes were made in 1987. Set in the showbusiness world and starring Mayall as an actor, Edmondson as his minder and Planer as his manager, the series in similar in humour and content to the Young Ones.

Facts British About Sitcoms

The world's first sitcom was Pinwright's Progress. This consisted of ten episodes and was broadcast between 29th November 1946-16th May 1947. The show was broadcast live so no recordings remain. It stars James Hayter as J. Pinwright who runs a small shop.

The first use of the term situation comedy was in a BBC memo dated 31st March 1953, It was used in regard to Hancock's Half Hour.

The first sitcom on British television not made by the BBC was The Army Game which first aired on 19 June 1957.

Last of the Summer Wine, which ran from 1973-2010, is the world's longest running sitcom.

The most exported British BBC sitcom is Keeping Up Appearances. It has been sold over a 1000 times to overseas broadcasters.

Fifty film versions of 45 British sitcoms have been made.

The Cambridge Dictionary describes a sitcom as:

 "a television series in which the same characters are involved in amusing situations in each show".

In 2003-2004 the BBC staged a poll to find

Britain's Best Sitcom. 100 were chosen. Then a 12 episode series on the top 10 sitcoms was shown with a live final to choose the winner.

The top ten sitcoms were:

Only Fools and Horses
Blackadder
The Vicar of Dibley
Dad's Army
Fawlty Towers
Yes Minister
Porridge
Open All Hours
The Good Life
One Foot in the Grave

British sitcoms have less episodes in a series (called seasons in the US) than their American counterparts. British sitcoms invariably have only 6 episodes per series, whereas American sitcoms have many more per year. This is because British sitcoms are often written by one or two people; in the US there is a team or writers.

The highest audience for a British sitcom episode of British television was the 1996 episode of Only Fools and Horses entitled Time on Our Hands, broadcast on the 29th December 1996. 24.3 million viewers watched. This was intended to be the final episode of the popular and long running sitcom, but it was brought back for three specials several years later.

Early in it's life, the sitcom was intended to be like
a theatre in a play. This is why it was filmed in
front of a live audience to try and recreate the
theatre experience for the viewer.